A Not So
Silent Night

DAILY READINGS DURING ADVENT

KIM BIASOTTO

FIRST EDITION

Cover art by Addi Gerlach, fourteen-year-old niece of author.
addigcreativity@gmail.Com

ISBN: 978-1-946466-25-9

Library of Congress Control Number: 2017952632

Published by

P.O. Box 2839, Apopka, FL 32704

Printed in the United States of America

A Not So Silent Night

DAILY READINGS DURING ADVENT

Silent night, holy night. All is calm, all is bright…

Really? Silent? Calm? I have a feeling the night Jesus was born was anything but calm and silent. But that's how life is, right? Busy, loud, hectic - especially this time of year. And yet in the middle of all this busy, crazy, running around - God is here. He is with us. Let's spend a few minutes each day this advent season with Him. Have a seat, pause for a moment and let's take a closer look at the time surrounding this Not So Silent Night.

Make Some Noise

Matthew 1:18–21

This is how the birth of Jesus the Messiah came about. His mother Mary was pledged to be married to Joseph, but before they came together, she was found to be pregnant through the Holy Spirit. Because Joseph her husband was faithful to the law, and yet did not want to expose her to public disgrace, he had in mind to divorce her quietly. But after he had considered this, an angel of the Lord appeared to him in a dream and said, "Joseph son of David, do not be afraid to take Mary home as your wife, because what is conceived in her is from the Holy Spirit. She will give birth to a son, and you are to give him the name Jesus because he will save his people from their sins."

Have you ever had a bad dream? Of course, you have. We all have. When we were younger, we often sought solace from our mom or dad. We ran to them for help. We made much noise as we explained our bad dream to them.

So, picture this. Here was Joseph, all ready to get married to Mary when he found out she was going to have a baby. He knew he was not the father, but he was a good man and didn't want to make a scene. He went to sleep one night and what did God do? He sent an angel to Joseph! Can you imagine having an angel visit you while you're sleeping? I don't know about you, but I don't think I could keep quiet, roll over, and go back to sleep!

Now the Bible doesn't tell us how Joseph reacted. It only says, "When Joseph woke up, he did what the angel of the Lord had commanded him and took Mary home as his wife" (Matthew 1:24). But I have to believe that between the time he saw the angel and got married, that man made some noise.

This Christmas season, don't be afraid to jump for joy, making some noise. Be watching what God is doing in and around you, and when you see it, give a shout of thanks. Clap your hands in praise. Dance around and thank God for His goodness, faithfulness, and forgiveness. Go ahead and make some noise!

Lord God, Thank You for Your goodness, Your faithfulness, and Your forgiveness. Thank You for the way You are working in me and around me. Help me to be quick to see You and praise You this Christmas season. Amen.

Greetings

Luke 1:26–33

God sent the angel Gabriel to Mary and said, "Greetings, you who are highly favored! The Lord is with you." Mary was greatly troubled at his words and wondered what kind of greeting this might be. But the angel said to her, "Do not be afraid, Mary; you have found favor with God."

The word *greetings* in this verse is like saying, *peace be with you* or *joy be with you.* It is a form of speech implying that she was important; therefore, Gabriel was expressing joy at meeting her.

Think about that for a minute. A word—a greeting—interrupted Mary's day. I have no idea what she was doing at the time. She could have been busy cooking, cleaning, or attending other daily chores. But all of a sudden, the angel Gabriel—whose name means *God is my strength*—appeared to Mary with much joy and excitement to see her.

Why?

He knew the Lord was with her; that she was the one God had chosen to carry His own Son to earth. She had found favor with God.

How cool is that?

This advent season, think about this when you're out and about in the crowded mall, the grocery store, at work, or in school where everyone is counting down the days until Christmas. With a few short words spoken out loud, Gabriel had made it clear that Mary was important to him and important to God. What words of greeting can you give someone to let them know they are important to you and important to God?

To the person sitting alone, a "hello and have a good day" can let them know someone sees them. To the mom struggling with a stroller and packages, a "hi, let me help you" can remind her she can do this. Be watching for ways God can use you to show people they are important to you and to God.

Greetings, God. Thank You for the reminder that You love to step into our days and encourage us. Please help me to interrupt someone's day with a greeting to show them that they are important to You and to me—not because of anything they've done or said, but because they were created by You and You love them! Amen.

Loud and Clear

Luke 2:1

In those days Caesar Augustus issued a decree that a census should be taken of the entire Roman world.

Have you ever been interrupted? You are sitting there, talking to a friend, and all of a sudden someone bursts into the room and starts talking. It is not always pleasant. It is not always subtle. It is NOT always quiet.

When we want to get someone's attention, we are often not subtle or quiet…and often not pleasant! Caesar Augustus, the Emperor of Rome, understood this. He needed a message to get out far and wide. Everyone was to return to their hometown to be counted and to pay their taxes. He sent that message loud and clear to the people. He was a powerful man, and when he spoke, the people listened and obeyed.

God is even more powerful. While sometimes He speaks loud and clear, other times He is that small, quiet voice that I can totally miss if I am not listening for it, especially this time of year. Can I hear Him above all the crowds and *fa-la-la-ing* and *ho-ho-ho-ing*? Can I hear Him above the shopping and wrapping and eating?

I can if I am still, if I pause and choose to listen, and if I take time out of this crazy, fun, busy season to wait on Him. It's my choice. Sometimes we are really good at it; and other times, not so much.

This advent season—in the midst of all the hustle and noise—pause. Listen. Spend time in the Word. What does God have for you today?

Heavenly Father, Thank You that I can come to You at any time! Help me to remember to pause and listen and spend time with You. Teach me to listen and hear and obey. Amen.

Pack Up and Move Out

Luke 2: 3–4

And everyone went to their own town to register. So Joseph also went up from the town of Nazareth in Galilee to Judea, to Bethlehem the town of David, because he belonged to the house and line of David. He went there to register with Mary, who was pledged to be married to him and was expecting a child.

Family vacations. There is nothing quite like them—car rides, hiking, boating, *Are we there yet?*, skiing, fishing, swimming, and *He's touching me!* Family vacations are wonderful things!

However, *preparing* for these wonderful family vacations is an entirely different matter—doing laundry, cleaning out the car, rushing out to buy goggles even though you had them three days ago and today they are nowhere to be found. Who will watch the dog? Who will feed the cat? Can the neighbors check our mail? Where is my rolling suitcase? Preparing for a vacation is NOT a quiet time.

Joseph and Mary were not going on vacation. However, they were planning a trip, along with many of their neighbors. Each man and his family had to head to the city of their birth to be counted and to pay taxes.

Food had to be made ahead, clothes had to be cleaned, and animals had to be cared for while they were gone. I imagine many households were anything but quiet during this time of preparation.

But that's life, isn't it? We are going along and all of a sudden something or someone out of the blue throws a wrench in our plans. We have to make a change, which can sometimes mean a lot of work, stress, and noise.

During this advent season, when something all of a sudden doesn't go like you thought it would, rest in the knowledge that this was not a surprise to God. He orders our days and is with us no matter what the day brings. Embrace the change. Make new memories. Enjoy the noise.

Dear God, Thank You that You are never surprised. Help me to embrace surprises and change as they occur and keep my heart and mind focused on You this Christmas season. Amen.

Swaddling Cloths

Luke 2:6–7

While they were there, the time came for the baby to be born, and she gave birth to her firstborn, a son and wrapped Him in swaddling cloths, and laid Him in a manger.

Nothing about having a baby is quiet. From the pains of delivery to the crying infant, from the "Whoop Whoop!" of the happy dad to the "Seriously, another girl?" from the big brother, having a baby brings many different reactions.

To comfort the crying infant, the Bible tells us that Mary wrapped Jesus in swaddling cloths. These are strips of cloth that are wrapped around the baby to make him feel safe and secure. Swaddling usually helps stop some of the tears. Unfortunately, we cannot stay swaddled in cloth our entire life. Eventually, we outgrow this as our need to stretch and explore outweighs the comfort of the cloth. Even though we outgrow the strips of cloth that once swaddled us, none of us outgrow our need to be comforted.

Psalm 33.32 says, "Let your unfailing love surround us, LORD, for our hope is in you alone."

God, our Father, knows this and offers Himself as our comforter.

As we surround ourselves in His Word and His promises, we will receive comfort.

Here are a few verses that offer hope and comfort.

The LORD himself goes before you and will be with you; he will never leave you nor forsake you. Do not be afraid; do not be discouraged. (Deuteronomy 31:8)

Even though I walk through the darkest valley, I will fear no evil, for you are with me; your rod and your staff, they comfort me. (Psalm 23:4)

Peace I leave with you; my peace I give you. I do not give to you as the world gives. Do not let your hearts be troubled and do not be afraid. (John 14:27)

When you get overwhelmed or on the verge of tears this advent season, go to the One who comforts. Wrap yourself in Him and His promises. He will not disappoint.

Jesus, You know what it is to be comforted. Please come and comfort us. Help us to remember Your promises and remind us that You are always with us. It's in your name we pray, Amen.

Bread Bed

Luke 2:6–7

While they were there, the time came for the baby to be born, and she gave birth to her firstborn, a son. She wrapped him in cloths and placed him in a manger because there was no guest room available for them.

Kids around the world sleep in all types of places—straw mats on the floor, hammocks hung in trees, sofas, beds, and even dresser drawers. We use what we have available to us. Jesus only had a manger to sleep in.

A manger is usually made of stone, wood or metal. It is a structure used to feed and water animals. The word manger literally means *to eat*.

Then Jesus declared, "I am the Bread of Life. Whoever comes to me will never go hungry, and whoever believes in me will never be thirsty." (John 6:35)

Jesus answered and said to her, "Everyone who drinks of this water will thirst again, but whoever drinks of the water that I will give him shall never thirst; but the water that I will give him will become in him a well of water springing up to eternal life." (John 4:13–14)

Think about this. There, surrounded by the noise of baaing sheep and mooing cows, God sent Jesus to earth to be the Bread of Life and the Living Water. The first place Jesus slept in was a bed that was designed to hold food and water! How cool is that? A manger is a place where animals eat and drink, producing strength to keep them alive. Jesus is the Living Water and the Bread of Life, and we are given this imagery on the first day that He is on this earth!

Whenever you see a nativity scene this Christmas, remember this marvelous bed that Jesus first slept in. Thank God for the gift of His Son and that He came to give us strength and life.

Dear God, Thank You for the great way You showed us that Jesus is here to meet our needs by letting him sleep in a manger bed. Help me be thankful for all You have given me. Amen.

Camping

Luke 2:8

And there were shepherds living out in the fields nearby, keeping watch over their flocks at night.

There are all sorts of people in this world. Some like to sit on the beach and swim in the ocean. Some like to ride horses and hike trails. Some like to climb mountains, and some even like to camp. There are different ways to camp using trailers, yurts, cabins, and tents. The variety is endless. One can camp in a field surrounded by many others, or in the woods all alone. Many people have a real love of camping.

The shepherds were **living** out in the fields while they watched over their flocks at night. This was hard-core camping. They had no pop-up trailer or fifth wheel with a waterbed. This was real outdoor life, whether it was rain or shine, hot or cold. There were no warm showers and no soft beds. While there was no traffic, radios for music, or noisy neighbors to keep them awake, they were surrounded by the different noises of bugs, birds, howling animals, and their sheep.

So why did they do this? It was their job. They are shepherds. That's what shepherds do. They lead the sheep to food and water. They help them grow and keep them safe.

I am the good shepherd. The good shepherd lays down his life for the sheep. (John 10:11)

Jesus **chooses** to be our good shepherd. It is not His job. It is His delight. He is there to provide what we need, to help us grow, and to keep us safe. And like these shepherds, Jesus is there day and night, rain or shine, good days or bad. He is there when we are quiet and when we are loud. He will never leave us! Read Psalm 121. It is a great place to be reminded how God is *always* with us.

This advent season, remember to thank God that He is *always* with us. When we are good or bad, happy, scared or sad, He will not leave us. He does not sleep and is always beside us.

Jesus, Thank You that You are with us day and night. You are always there to lead us and comfort us and protect us. Amen.

DECEMBER 8

All of a Sudden!

Luke 2:8–9

And there were shepherds living out in the fields nearby, keeping watch over their flocks at night. An angel of the Lord appeared to them.

Try this fun trick. All you need is a napkin, tissue or cloth of some kind, and your hand.

Make a fist with one hand.

Hold up your pointer finger.

Cover your pointer finger with the cloth.

Say something funny like wiggly-woggly.

As you lift the cloth with a flourish, quickly pull your pointer finger back down into your fist.

Amazing. You made it disappear.

It can be easy to make things disappear. Whether it's nachos at a football party or a puddle evaporating in the sun, things seem to more often go from *here* to *not here*. It is much harder, and less common, to have something suddenly appear, going from nothing to something.

Imagine what it was like for the shepherds. There they were out in the field with stars in the sky and sheep snoring loudly. When all of a sudden, there in the sky, an angel of the Lord appeared. If things had been quiet, they weren't now. Shouts of surprise, fear, and astonishment suddenly filled the air. I bet even the sheep had a thing or two to say. They were surely baaa-wildered!

The Bible tells us that the shepherds were *keeping watch over their sheep.* Maybe this is one reason why they were so *very* surprised. Instead of keeping their eyes on things above, their focus was on the things around them. I realize their job was to watch the sheep, but how many times when we are busy doing our job, going to school, or walking the dog that we forget to look up expectantly, waiting, watching, and hoping to see God move?

If you can, pause for a moment and look up at the sky. What do you see? Clouds? The sun? Stars? Snow? Rain? Angels? No matter what you see, hold your gaze there for a minute. Keep looking up toward the One who came down. Look up toward the One who chose to step into time, to be born in a barn, sleep in a manger, live as a man, and die on a cross. He came when He was not expected, but dearly and desperately hoped for.

This advent season, regularly take the time to pause and look up to remember that the God who is above, came down. Remember He wants to be a part of our day. He longs to show up and in an instant, make something out of nothing.

Lord God, Thank You for being an amazing and surprising God who loves to make something out of nothing. Help me to remember to pause and look up, waiting and watching for You. Amen.

Preview

Luke 2:8–9

And there were shepherds living out in the fields nearby, keeping watch over their flocks at night. An angel of the Lord appeared to them, and the glory of the Lord shone around them, and they were terrified.

Proverbs 9:10–11 tells us,

The fear of the LORD is the beginning of wisdom, and knowledge of the Holy One is understanding. For through wisdom your days will be many, and years will be added to your life.

Based on these verses, the shepherds were going to be super wise really fast and live a long time. They were experiencing some serious fear of the Lord! But as terrifying, noisy, and unsettling as the appearance of the angel was to them, I imagine they had no idea their fear was only the beginning of their wisdom. This was their first introduction to the Holy One.

How many times do we see God do something great and we say, "Yay!" and "Thanks!" and move on? In reality, God's moving was just the *beginning* of our wisdom? What if, in reality, the things we experience are the great preview of even greater things to come? What would happen if after we experienced God's greatness, we pressed in, waited, and watched for more? Maybe His moving is like the grand announcement He gave to the shepherds when He said, "Get ready for this guys. It is going to blow your mind!" [Paraphrased]

It would be like winning $100,000 a year for life and only picking up the first installment. Yes, that $100,000 would be awesome and we could do so much with it, but it would only be a great preview of even more money to come.

This advent season, watch for God to move in mighty ways and then draw even closer to Him. Let it be the beginning of your wisdom. Like the shepherds, we have no idea what is coming next; but I, for one, don't want to miss it!

Dear God, Thank You that You are the Good Shepherd who loves His sheep and the good Father who loves to do great things for His kids. Help us watch and wait and press in when we see You. Help us to continually grow in wisdom. Amen.

Glory

Luke 2:9

An angel of the Lord appeared to them, and the glory of the
Lord shone around them, and they were terrified.

On this most likely cold day in December, take a moment and
picture yourself sitting on the beach. The sun is warm. Your
chair is at the edge of the sea. You sit and gaze out over the water. Soon,
you are getting hot so you decide to take a dip. The water is cool and
refreshing.

It is glorious.

Suddenly, out of nowhere, a large wave appears and you get
slammed. One minute you are standing there, toes in the sand, waist
deep in water; and the next minute you are being tossed head over heels
in the surf. Which way is up? How do I find my bearings? What do I
do now? This ocean—that a moment ago was giving you such peaceful
refreshment—can, in an instant, throw you for a loop. Literally.

I have a feeling this was how the shepherds felt when the angel
appeared and they were surrounded by the glory of the Lord. The peace
of the night was shattered. The stars and the moon that shone brightly

were instantly overshadowed by the greatness of God. The shepherds were thrown for a loop—probably quite literally.

This advent season, let us not forget the greatness of the glory of God. The God who shapes each snowflake also constructs the lightning. The God who created the crocus molded the mountains. He is the God that the waves and the wind obey. He is the God who holds the world in His hands. This can seem frightening, but I challenge you to see it as encouragement. There is *nothing* our God cannot handle. He is bigger and greater and mightier than *all* things. Let us never forget that.

Almighty God, I am thankful that You are strong and powerful and can do all things. Remind me to come to You when I don't know which way is up, when I need to find my bearings, and when I just don't know what to do. Thank You that You love me and want the best for me. In Jesus' name, Amen.

Merry Christmas

Luke 2:10

But the angel said to them, "Do not be afraid. I bring you good news that will cause great joy for all the people."

Who doesn't love a holiday or festival? They are noisy, joyous events full of food, family, friends, and traditions. Holidays happen all over the world throughout the entire year. How many of these holidays have you heard of?

Passover: A holiday or festival celebrated by Jewish people. They celebrate it to remember when God protected His people as the angel of death flew over.

Ramadan: A special month of the year when Muslims do not eat between sunrise and sunset. It is a time of reflection; a time to think about those less fortunate and draw closer to God.

Memorial Day: A United States holiday to remember those who have served in our armed forces. It's often celebrated with flags, parades, and picnics.

Diwali: The "Festival of Lights" in India where people place clay lamps and lights outside their homes to symbolize the inner light that protects them from spiritual darkness.

What is one thing that all these holidays have in common? They are each celebrated by a group of people within a nation or nationality. How, you may ask, is this any different than Christmas? Isn't the real meaning of Christmas a time for Christians to celebrate the birth of Christ?

Yes, it is. But it is so much more. Look at today's verse again.

But the angel said to them, "Do not be afraid. I bring you good news that will cause great joy for all the people."

Christmas is for *all* people. The news that Jesus is born isn't just for the shepherds, or just for the Jews, or just for the Christians. It is good news that will cause great joy for *all* people.

Jesus came to seek and to save the lost—*all* of us! Those who celebrate Passover, Ramadan, Memorial Day, and Diwali need to hear the good news of Christmas, too.

This advent season is a great time to share the good news of Jesus. As you are out celebrating, eating food, and making noise, tell someone *why* you are celebrating and invite them to join in. After all, Christmas is for everyone.

Jesus, Thank You that You came to earth with a plan to save EVERYONE. Show me how I can share this truth with the people I come in contact with this season. Help me share this good news with great joy. Amen.

DECEMBER 12

Today

Luke 2:11

"Today in the town of David a Savior has been born to you; he is the Messiah, the Lord."

If you knew that Jesus was returning today, would that change the way you spent your day? Would it change the way you behaved today? Would you be nicer? Would you help more people across the street or share your toys?

A lot can happen in one day. I am sure when the shepherds got up that morning they thought, "Ho, hum, just another day in the fields with the sheep." They had no idea what the day was going to bring. They had NO idea that their savior, their Messiah, was going to be born that day.

But what if they had known? Do you think they would have acted any differently? Would they have been kinder to each other or given the sheep an extra portion of food? I imagine they would not have sat quietly as they waited. They would have scurried around talking with each other. "How do I look?" "I am so sorry for stealing your crook last month!" "I will lead the sheep to water today." "We need to get ready!"

Did you know Jesus' last sermon on earth was about being ready for His return? Read Matthew 25. He talks about the ten virgins. Five are ready; five are not. He talks about separating the sheep from the goats. He reminds the people to feed the hungry, clothe the naked, attend to the sick, invite the strangers in, and visit the prisoners. Doing these things for others is like doing these things for Him.

There are twenty-seven books in the New Testament. In twenty-three of them, Jesus talks about coming again. There are over three hundred references to this! This is not to be overlooked or ignored.

In thirteen days we celebrate Jesus' first setting foot on earth as a man. Let's live this advent season as if today is the day He is returning. Let's keep our eyes upward, minister to those around us, and pray that today is the day He returns.

Jesus, Thank You for coming to earth as a baby. Thank You that You are coming again. Help me to live in a way that when You come again, I am found ready and waiting and pleasing to you. Amen.

Choose Your Family

Luke 2:11

"Today in the town of David a Savior has been born to you; he is the Messiah, the Lord."

Bethlehem, the town of David, was a city located about five miles south of Jerusalem. King Saul and King David were both born here and David died here. Samuel anointed David here and told him one day he would be king. The love story of Ruth and Boaz took place in Bethlehem. This is where Jacob's beloved wife Rachel is buried. It is one of the oldest cities in the world. In Hebrew, Bethlehem means *house* (or place) *of bread.* Cool, right? The Bread of Life was born in the *house of bread* [Bethlehem] and then placed in a *bread bed* [manger].

Where are you from? What city were you born in? No matter where it was—Wilmington, Warsaw, or Wiesbaden—God was there, too. He knit you together. He made you, formed you, and smiled with pride when you were born. You were made in His image. He has a plan for you, for good and not for evil, with a future and a hope! He heard your first cry and every cry you've made since.

God loves all your noises—your loud, "I am so happy" cheers, your "Why did this happen?" questions, and your "Will it ever stop hurting?" pleas. Just as He was in Bethlehem for the birth of Jesus, He was also at your birth, smiling down and rejoicing that you were now a part of this world.

It has been said that you can't choose your family, but you can choose your friends. In a way, this is true. You are born to a mom and dad, and you have *no* control over who they are. You can, however, choose to be a part of God's family. It is a gift he freely offers. God is not going to force you to become a part of His family.

If you have not chosen to be a part of God's family, could there be a better time than this advent season to do so? It's the time of year when we celebrate Jesus stepping into the earth. This season is the perfect time for you to choose to step into His family, too. He is waiting with open arms to say, "Welcome my child, I have been waiting for you."

Jesus, Thank You for coming at Christmas. Thank You for making a way for us to become a part of Your family by taking the punishment for us. Help me to honor and reflect You with all I do or ask or think. Amen.

DECEMBER 14

Ask, Seek, Knock

Luke 2:12

"This will be a sign to you: You will find a baby wrapped in cloths and lying in a manger."

I love the angel's message here. The Messiah is born, today, just west of here in the *house of bread* [Bethlehem]. You will know which baby it is because he will be the one wrapped in cloth and sleeping in a feeding trough. How great is that? How crazy is that? The angel didn't say "go to 123 Manger Street" or "look for the place with the big red door with a wreath on it." He said, "Go now to Bethlehem. You *will* find the baby in the manger."

That seems like such a monumental task. Look around in the city until you find this particular baby. This goes right along with what Jesus will be teaching one day. Just a few pages ahead in our Bible, Jesus tells his disciples, "Ask, and it will be given to you; seek, and you will find; knock, and the door will be opened to you. For everyone who asks receives; he who seeks finds; and to him who knocks, the door will be opened" (Luke 11:9–10).

Jesus says, "Ask, seek, knock." In other words, make some noise. "If you want to find Me, I am here. I promise if you are looking, I *will* be found." I have a feeling that is what these shepherds did. They asked, they sought, and they knocked on doors until they found the one they were seeking. In the middle of that *not so silent night*, they made some noise.

This advent season, ask, seek, knock. Ask God to reveal His Son to you in new ways. Seek Jesus in the midst of the crazy, the chaos, and the fun. Knock on the door of heaven with your prayers and thank God for the gift of His Son. For everyone who asks, receives; he who seeks, finds; and to him who knocks, the door will be opened.

Thank You, Jesus, for Your promise that if we seek You, we will find You. Help us to seek You in this busy time of year, to watch for the ways you are moving, and to thank You for doing abundantly above all we could ask or think. Amen.

Independence Day

Luke 2:13–14

Suddenly a great company of the heavenly host appeared with the angel, praising God and saying, "Glory to God in the highest heaven, and on earth peace to those on whom his favor rests."

July Fourth is a great, fun holiday full of picnics with deviled eggs, charbroiled burgers, Grandma's potato salad, and lots of noise. Pool parties are complete with egg tosses and noodle races. Parades are full of streamer-clad bikes ridden by kids waving flags, homemade floats, and ending with the piercing wail of the fire trucks. As fun as that is, it is nothing compared to what happens when the sun goes down. People bring out their chairs and blankets and lift their faces skyward as they wait with anticipation for the fireworks to begin. Sometimes, it feels like *forever* before the first firework lights up the night sky. Once it does, you are surrounded with "oooh's and aah's." Some fireworks are huge; others make pictures in the sky. Some fireworks have almost no light, but make a stomach-churning *boom*. This is a fantastic holiday.

We do all this on July Fourth to celebrate our country's freedom. We celebrate our freedom from Britain's rule as an independent nation.

That is why we call it Independence Day.

Now let your mind wander back to the night the shepherds were out with their sheep. An angel appeared to them and freaked them out. He told them good news. The Messiah had been born. And then, as if one angel wasn't enough, hundreds—or even thousands—of angels lit up the night sky, praising God! They made some *crazy* noise, I'm sure. I can't imagine how incredible that was. It must have been like a live heavenly firework show, exceedingly cooler than any show we have ever seen! (On a side note, if one angel frightened the shepherds, imagine what this was like!)

In a way, this was the start of Independence Day for Christians. The birth of Jesus made a way for us to be *free* from the punishment of sin. Jesus made it possible for us to be liberated from Satan's rule and become part of God's family.

This advent season, rejoice in your independence as a nation and as a believer. Lift your face skyward. Imagine what it must have been like when the angels filled the sky, and thank God for sending His Son so we can be truly free!

Dear God, I cannot imagine what it was like on that night. Thank You for sending Your angels with the good news that Jesus was born and for making a way for us to become a part of Your family. Amen.

Listen Then Obey

Luke 2:15

When the angels had left them and gone into heaven, the shepherds said to one another, "Let's go to Bethlehem and see this thing that has happened, which the Lord has told us about."

This is a great verse. It does **not** say, "When the angels left, the shepherds looked at each other and said, "SERIOUSLY? What was that?" It also does **not** say, "The shepherds then had a snack and went back to watching their sheep." It basically says the shepherds responded by saying, "We need to go to Bethlehem and check this out." No arguing. No "I will do it later." No making a five-step plan. They just did it.

Why do you think they acted this way? I am going to say at least one reason is that they knew the message was from God who had authority over them. They listened and obeyed. God will often ask us to do things and just wants us to listen and obey. He does not make deals: "If you do this, I will give you a cookie." He will not always explain why: "You need to clean your room because Aunt Betty is coming over and she doesn't have kids. She doesn't understand why we need all this stuff, and she really does not like a mess."

Advent season can be a crazy, busy time with lots to do, see, eat, attend, and buy. When someone with authority asks us to do something, we are often quick to come up with a reason not to do it. I am *not* saying this means we should jump and say *yes* to every request that comes along. If that were the case, you would be doing all kinds of things that you don't need to do. What I am saying is consider *who* is asking and what they want you to do. If they are in authority, and not asking you to go against God's rules, listen and obey.

Are your parents asking you to clean up your toys? They are your parents. They have authority. Listen and obey. Is your boss asking for help on something? He or she is your boss. They have authority. Listen and obey.

In doing this, we are blessing others and forming a good habit so when God asks something of us, we just listen and obey.

God, help me to be quick to listen, and willing to obey You and those in authority over me. In Jesus' name, I pray, Amen.

Widgets and Thingamabobs

Luke 2:16

So they hurried off and found Mary and Joseph, and the baby, who was lying in the manger.

What do you do when you are trying to open a jar of pickles, jelly, or chocolate spread and you just can't get the lid off? If you are like me, you twist one more time and accompany it with a noisy grunt. When that doesn't work, I try and find someone stronger than I am. But if that said strong person is not around, and that creamy chocolate is calling, I grab a jar opening widget and use it to unlock the sugary goodness.

When my jar opening widget is not in use, it sits in a drawer with numerous other handy thingamabobs, each designed to complete a specific task. They are not used often, but when they are, they are just what is needed to do the job and do it well.

Now let's look at Joseph. We first met Joseph in the book of Luke when we are told he was pledged to Mary. Next time we hear about him is when he and Mary were heading to the little town of Bethlehem. Joseph was there with mother and baby when the shepherds came to visit.

Joseph does not play a major role in Scripture. He doesn't fight a giant, heal the sick, or part the Red Sea. We have no stories of Joseph dining with queens or hanging with lepers. This does *not* mean that Joseph was unimportant. He is like the widget in the drawer—designed with a specific purpose—to help raise Jesus, the Son of God. Out of all the men living at that time, God chose Joseph to be by Mary's side. He was chosen to help teach young Jesus to walk, to talk, and to be a part of the community. He cared for Him and taught Him a trade as a carpenter.

It can be so easy to compare ourselves to *super Christians*. You know who I mean. They are the ones that lead and teach and sing. They are in the public eye. We look at them and think, "Wow, God must really be proud of them." But look at Joseph. He was not in the public eye. He was the *thingamabob* in the drawer, ready for when God called him. When He did, Joseph was used to play a huge part in raising Jesus.

This advent season, be willing make some noise leading or teaching, or singing, or just sitting still like a widget or thingamabob in the drawer. Be ready for when God calls you to do something. Like with Joseph, it could happen in an instant! God made you with a plan and a purpose.

Dear God, Thank You for the people who are out front and center and point us to You. Thank You for the widgets in the drawer who are ready and willing to serve You. Show me each day how You want to use me and help me to be ready when You call. Amen.

DECEMBER 18

Hearing is Believing

Luke 2:17–18

When they had seen him, they spread the word concerning what had been told them about this child, and all who heard it were amazed at what the shepherds said to them.

This time of year we are inundated with noisy commercials of things we MUST have to make us complete… toys, jewels, lotions, electronics, and even vehicles.

"She walks, and talks, and even wets her diaper. Your little girl NEEDS *Baby Be Real*!"

"Just slather *Youth in a Bottle* cream over your entire body and ALL your wrinkles will disappear before your eyes. It's miraculous! It can be yours for just four easy payments of $39.99."

We are told if we really love someone, we must spend a fortune to show them the depths and sincerity of our affections. Does it work? Look under most Christmas trees on December 25th in this country, and you tell me.

In today's verse, the shepherds had just seen Jesus in the flesh. The baby that the angels told them about moments before was right before their eyes. What do they do next? They left and spread the word.

But keep reading. They spread the word concerning what they had been *told* about this child.

By the word of the LORD the heavens were made, their starry host by the breath of his mouth. (Psalm 33:6)

With the spoken word, Satan was thrown aside.
Jesus said to him, "Away from me, Satan! For it is written: Worship the Lord your God, and serve him only." (Matthew 4:10)

With the spoken word, the winds and the waves were still.
He got up, rebuked the wind and said to the waves, "Quiet! Be still!" Then the wind died down and it was completely calm. (Mark 4:39)

There is power in the spoken word.
With a spoken word, the heavens and the earth were created.

The angels told the shepherds about the birth of the Son of God being born. They believed and then passed on what they had been told. They spoke and told others.

This advent season, listen to the words being spoken around you. Ask God to help you discern truth from lies. Watch your words. Speak the truth in love. Encourage each other. Build each other up and spread the word about what the angels told the shepherds. Jesus was born!

Lord God, there are so many things said this time of year. Show me what to listen to and what to ignore. Help me to watch the words that come out of my mouth. Help me to speak only kind words that build people up. If I do speak unkind words, help me to be quick to ask forgiveness from the offended and from You. Thank You for the power of your words! Amen.

Buried Treasure

Luke 2:19

But Mary treasured up all these things and pondered them in her heart.

Imagine you are walking along the surf and a glass bottle drifts toward your feet. You pick it up. It is old and sealed with a cork. You open it up to find a piece of paper inside. Wait, it is more than a piece of paper. It is a treasure map complete with a big red X that marks a special spot. You grab some buddies and a shovel and before long, you've unearthed a treasure chest! What do you think is inside? A treasure, of course, of gold and jewels and crowns. You are elated.

Why do people bury treasure? There are probably lots of reasons. To hide it. To keep it safe. To put it in a place only you know so you can come back to it later.

The nine months before Jesus was born, Mary had a lot going on. She was pledged to marry Joseph, was visited by an angel, told she was going to have God's son, traveled to Bethlehem, had the baby, and was visited by shepherds while Jesus was lying in a manger. Instead of freaking out and making a bunch of noise (like everyone around her), we are told time and time again that she accepted and pondered and treasured what was happening.

I like that it is written, "Mary treasured up all these things." Picture it. Mary put all the thoughts, feelings, and emotions of what she was experiencing—the surprise of the angel, Joseph's kindness, the long trip to Bethlehem, having a baby who slept in a feeding trough—in her heart like they were treasures in a chest. Then she could bury that chest in her mind so that at any time she wanted, she could dig it up, open the box, and remember all these things with amazement.

This advent season, watch for ways God gives you treasure. Did you do something fun with a family member? Bury this memory like treasure in your mind so you can come back to it later and remember and smile. Did you attend a moving concert, read a great book, see a light display that inspired you? Picture yourself putting this as treasure in a chest and bury it in your mind, knowing you can come back to it and enjoy the memory of this special time.

Jesus, Thank You for allowing us to experience good times with pleasing memories. Help us to watch for the treasure You send our way and to treasure these things as gifts from You. Amen.

Changed

Luke 2:20

The shepherds returned, glorifying and praising God for all the things they had heard and seen, which were just as they had been told.

One week from today you can breathe easy. The gifts will be unwrapped. The Christmas turkey will be soup. The relatives will be back at home and the kids will be bored with their new toys. Life will return to *normal*. That's one thing we know about life; it keeps moving on. Good, bad, cold, warm—life is constantly changing.

In a short time span, the shepherds experienced a lot. They were startled by angels, excited to see the baby, outspoken as they told people far and near what they had heard, and now, they were full of joy as they returned to their fields and their sheep. They had a crazy couple of days. Their life had changed in ways they could not have anticipated. It's safe to say, they were changed as well. They had experienced God face to face; there was no way they could be the same.

I wish that around Luke, chapter 9, the shepherds were revisited. Years had gone by. What were they up to now? Did they still talk about that night? Did they continue to watch Jesus as He grew? Follow Him as he taught? Were they among the 5000 that He fed? Did they see Him heal the blind or raise Lazareth? And years from now, would their grandchildren be telling stories about how their relatives had seen the Messiah?

Unfortunately, we just don't know. I like to imagine at least a few of them watched Jesus grow, heard Him teach and continued to follow Him. However, from personal experience, I know how fast we can come down from a *Jesus high* and go back to life, as we know it.

This advent season, when you see God move, when you learn something new, when He speaks to you and you are changed—even a little bit—savor it. Learn from it. Notate it, write it down so you can go back to it. The feelings that accompany your experience won't last, but make the impact of your experience last. Ask God to write it on your heart and keep it in your mind. This way as your life keeps changing, you will have a constant reminder from the One who does not change.

Dear God, I thank You that You do not change. Help me to follow You and stay close to You so when You move I am changed and made more and more like You. In Jesus' name, Amen.

Names

Luke 2:21

On the eighth day, when it was time to circumcise the child, he was named Jesus. This was the name the angel had given him before he was conceived.

Do you know what your name means? If your name is Thomas, it means *Twin*; Amy means *Dearly Loved*; Robert means *Shining*; Martha means *Lady;* and Daniel means *God is my Judge*.

I love names. They tell a story. They have a history. They have significance.

The angel told Mary she was going to have a son and she was to name him Jesus (or *Yeshua* in Hebrew, *YehSou* in Cantonese, or *Yesu* in Swahili). Regardless of the language, the meaning is the same—*The Lord is Salvation*. Before the Son of Man was even conceived, He was to be known as *The Lord is Salvation*.

But Jesus was called many things!
Emmanuel: *God is with us*
Christ: *Anointed One*
Rabbi: *Teacher, Master*

There are so many names for Jesus because there are so many facets to Him—*Lamb of God, Light of the World, Savior, Messiah, Redeemer, King of Kings, Lord of Lords,* and *Prince of Peace,* to name a few more. There is not one name that can encapsulate all of who He is; each name we use gives us only a glimpse of who He is.

Let this encourage you. Jesus can meet us right where we are. He is just who we need at any certain moment. Do you need a teacher, comforter, savior, or a peace giver? Good. He is all of these. Call out to Him and lean on Him. He is the name above all names. He knows what you need and loves you.

This advent season, learn and use a new name for Jesus, or learn how to say Jesus in a different language. Talk to Him with this name. It is a great reminder of how huge and mighty and diverse He is. He is whatever we need, whenever we need Him.

Dear ___[Fill in a new name for Jesus]___, Thank You that You are here for me no matter what I need. Help me to turn to You whenever I need to. Remind me that there is nothing You cannot handle. In Your mighty and powerful name, I pray, Amen.

DECEMBER 22

May I Present...

Luke 2:22

When the time came for the purification rites required by the Law of Moses, Joseph and Mary took him to Jerusalem to present him to the Lord.

*M**a 'chere Mademoiselle,*
It is with deepest pride and greatest pleasure that we welcome you tonight.

And now we invite you to relax, let us pull up a chair as the dining room proudly presents your dinner!

Do you recognize this quote?

The talking candlestick, Lumiere, said this just before Belle was entertained by her magical meal in Disney's *Beauty and the Beast*. The dishes danced, the food spun, and the drink shoots from a fountain. Belle is mesmerized, trying to take it all in.

When Joseph and Mary brought Jesus to Jerusalem, it was hardly the same setting as the magical movie castle. However, they went to Jerusalem to present something as well. Instead of a spinning meal, He was someone who would one day feed five thousand people. Instead of a shooting fountain drink, He was the One who would be known as the *Living Water*.

They came to present Jesus to God.

Think about that. They went to Jerusalem to dedicate Jesus to the service of God, offering Him to God in a formal way. Can you picture Joseph saying, "God, I would like to present Jesus to You? I know He is Your Son, but we want You to know we are going to do our best to raise Him in a way that will please you."

What I like even better is to picture God looking down, smiling as He says, "Yes, that is my child. Thank you for being there with him. Here we go. This is going to be…awesome, hard, encouraging, frightening, powerful, mind blowing…" It is mesmerizing, just trying to take it all in.

This advent season, what can you present to God? After all, it is a time of presents. What do you have that you can give to God? It doesn't have to be a tangible item, but it can be. Are you willing to put a little more in the offering plate to help people who have next to nothing? Are you willing to send money to a missionary as a surprise blessing? Can you give that extra coat, pair of shoes, hat, or car to someone who needs it? Maybe instead of a physical thing, it can be something inside of you. Can you give God your attitude and allow him to change and shape it? Your anger? Your greed? Your overeating (which is SO hard this time of year)?

When you do present something to God, picture Him looking down on you, saying, "Yes! That is *My* child. Here we go. This is going to be…awesome, hard, encouraging, frightening, powerful, mind blowing…" It is mesmerizing, just trying to take it all in.

God, Thank You for the many ways you have blessed me. Let me present my _____ to you to use as you see fit. Thank You for the gift of Jesus. It's in His name I pray, Amen.

Some Assembly Required

Luke 2:39

When Joseph and Mary had done everything required by the
Law of the Lord, they returned to Galilee to their own town
of Nazareth.

Some assembly required. These words can make one laugh or
cry, depending on how much is *some*. It could mean slip tab
A into slot B and be finished. Or, it could mean you gather your allen
wrench, socket set, phillips head screwdriver, needle nose pliers, and
turn to page 1 of the enclosed ninety-seven-page instruction manual!
Often, we have no idea how much work a job is going to entail until we
actually start the job; and even then, things can pop up to complicate the
task. "So *which* wire goes here?" "Wait, the big tire goes on the *front* of
the bike?" "It needs *how many* D cell batteries?" If we knew up front
how much work something was going to take, there would be a good
chance we wouldn't even try to do it.

Mary and Joseph headed home. The shepherds were back living
in their fields. The angels no longer lit up the sky. The manger was now
filled with fresh hay, and these new parents were making the journey
back to Nazareth. While some noises had ended, each day forward

would continue to be filled with all sorts of new sounds—laughter, as Jesus tried to say *Mama*; cheers, as He took his first steps; coughing, when He got sick; and singing, when Jesus needed comforting.

Jesus' parents had no idea what lie ahead, but they took one day at a time doing all they could to obey God and raise Jesus to the best of their ability. God walked them through life as He molded them into loving parents, good friends, and kind neighbors—the people He designed them to be. They didn't start out the same as they ended. They grew day-by-day, month-by-month, year-by-year, and faced each new day as it came.

Aren't you glad we don't know what each day is going to bring? If we did, there's a chance we wouldn't even try to get out of bed, saying, "Today is going to be too hard, too sad, too busy, or too boring."

But aren't you also glad that God knows exactly what each day is going to bring? He goes before us to make sure there is a way when there seems to be no way. As we go through each day, He gives us a chance to become more and more like Him. He wants to mold us into the people He designed us to be.

This advent season, when the days seems too hard or sad or busy or boring, remember whatever is happening is no surprise to God. When you think, "I can't do this," remember God is always at work. He is with you, using whatever happens in your day to build you, shape you, and mold you more and more into His image. In addition, He has given us a manual that we can read for help—His Word. It may not always be easy, but with God, it is always possible.

Dear God, Thank You that Christmas is almost here. When I have a day that is really not going the way I want it to, help me to remember that You know and care and are here with me. Help me to go to the Bible for instruction. Thank You that You make all things possible and every day new. Please make me more and more like You. In Jesus' name, Amen.

Silent Night

Silent Night, Holy Night, All is calm, All is bright
Round yon virgin Mother and child. Holy infant so tender and
mild. Sleep in heavenly peace, Sleep in heavenly peace.
(Text: Joseph Mohr, 1816. Melody: Franz Xaver Gruber, 1818)

Silent Night was first performed on Christmas Eve in 1818 in a town near Salzburg, Austria. Tradition has said that hungry church mice had eaten through the organ's bellows in St. Nicholas Church and there was no time or money to have them fixed for the Christmas Eve mass. Joseph Mohr, the assistant pastor, did not want a service with no music so he approached Franz Grube and gave him a poem he had written two years before. Mohr asked Gruber to write a melody for it to be played on the guitar. Franz Gruber completed the task and that night, the world heard for the first time, the song we know as *Silent Night*.

It has been estimated that this song has been translated into over 140 languages. During both World War I and World War II, it has been recorded that—on more than one occasion—fighting at Christmas was halted as troops from both sides sang this song across enemy borders.

The advent season is coming to an end. And while you still may be hanging stockings with care, attending church services, and assembling toys, I encourage you to take some time to be silent. Sit and be still and marvel at the events you are about to celebrate. Remember that God sent His Son into this loud, crazy, noisy, mixed up, messed up world for you.

No matter where you find yourself this December 24, know that God is with you.

No matter what noises surround you—little ones crying, choirs singing, IV machines beeping, families laughing, tummy's growling, or TV's telling you, it's a wonderful life—*this* is the world Jesus came to save. You are the one Jesus came to save.

This baby—fully God and completely boy, born to a teenager, placed in a feeding trough, heralded by angels, visited by shepherds, and raised by a carpenter—started as an infant and grew in strength and wisdom.

This worker of miracles, raiser of Lazareth, feeder of the masses, and partier with sinners, never sinned.

This Son of the Most High died in pain, was buried in a rock, defeated death, and rose in power!

Why? For you…so you can have a relationship with God!

Celebrate, rejoice, and remember all of this on this ***not so silent, holy night.***

Happy Birthday, Jesus. Thank You for coming to earth for us. Thank You that we can celebrate Your birth. Thank You that in all of this noise, we can stop and remember and rejoice. In your name we pray, Amen.

About the Author

Kim Biasotto is a speaker and writer who lives in Wilmington, Delaware. She is grateful for her supportive, loving husband, her four extraordinary children and her new son-in-law who embraces this families' eccentricities, laughter, and noise remarkably well.